Longman Group Limited
Longman House,
Burnt Mill, Harlow, Essex, CM20 2JE, England
and Associated Companies throughout the World

First published 1983

ISBN 0 582 25057 9 (Into the past 10, 11 & 12: Cased edition)
ISBN 0 582 18781 8 (10. Children in the Second World War — Paper edition)
ISBN 0 582 18782 6 (11. At home in the 1950s — Paper edition)
ISBN 0 582 18783 4 (12. At school in the 1950s — Paper edition)

Set in 12/18 pt. Univers

Printed in Hong Kong by
Astros Printing Ltd.

Acknowledgements

We are grateful to the following for permission to reproduce photographs:

Children in the Second World War
BBC Hulton Picture Library, facing page 1, pages 2, 5, 12 above, 13 and 23; Fox Photos, pages 3, 16, 24 and front cover above left; Imperial War Museum, pages 12 below, 14 below, 17 and 19; Institute of Agricultural History and Museum of English Rural Life, University of Reading, page 14 above; Popperfoto, pages 10 above left, 11, 15, 20, 21 and 22; The Tank Museum, page 6; Southern Newspapers, pages 7, 8, 9, and 10 below right; D.C. Thompson and Co, page 18; John Topham Picture Library, pages 4 and back cover above right; Trades Union Congress, page 1.

At home in the 1950s
BBC Hulton Picture Library, pages 3, 10, 12, 14, 15, 16, 18, 20, 21 above, front cover above right and back cover below; BBC, pages 7, 8 below left and 9; Cambridgeshire Libraries (Cambridgeshire Collection), pages 1 and 13; Harlow Council, pages 2, 4, 22–3 and 24; Pye, pages 6 and 8 above right; Science Museum, London, page 11.
Photographs on pages 5, 17 and 21 below are by Gwil Owen.
The compact on page 5 was kindly lent by Museum on a Shoestring.

At school in the 1950s
Albrighton County Junior School, page 22; Basildon Development Corporation, page 4 above; BBC Hulton Picture Library, pages 10 above and 16; Henry Grant, page 19; Greater London Council Photograph Library, pages 1, 3, 6, 10 below, 17 and back cover above left; Jacqueline Guy, page 7; Barry Jones, pages 4 below, 20, 21 and front cover below; Popperfoto, pages 5 and 11; Ann Samuel, page 9; Raphael Tuck and Sons, page 2.
Photographs on pages 12 and 23 left are by Gwil Owen.

Children in
the Second World War

Elizabeth Merson

Longman

To the reader

This book will help you to go back in time: from the present into the past. When you have read a page, you will find some "Things to do". You can make a book of your own about children in the war, life at home and going to school in the 1950s.

Talk to someone over 40 who remembers the war and the 1950s. They may be able to tell you what it was like 40 and 30 years ago. Have a list of questions you want to ask them. Collect your answers on a tape recorder or in writing. Tell your friends what you find out.

Try to borrow some things that people used during the war. Here are some things you may be able to collect: photographs, ration books, medals, badges and gas masks. Or you can have an exhibition of things from the home and school in the 1950s. You might be able to collect plastic objects, clothes, records, school reports, books or newspaper cuttings.

Some museums, shops and market stalls display things which were used in the war or at home and at school in the 1950s. See if you can find any.

All the sentences in **"bold type"** in this book
are the things people remembered about the war,
life at home and school 30 years ago.
The words are exactly what they said.

Press photographers looked like this over 30 years ago.
These photographers were eager
to get photographs for their newspapers.

Contents

Canterbury, Kent 1942

Preparing for war

On 1 September 1939 thousands of school children said goodbye to their parents. Everyone expected a war to start, so the children were sent to safer places in the country.

London 1940

"We were told to turn up at school with a packed lunch,
a change of clothes, and our gas masks.
I had a brown label tied to my coat.
I was six when I went away. I had never left home before."

Look at the children lining up to go on the train.
Look for:

—the labels with the children's names and addresses
—the caps and berets
—the girl holding her packed lunch tied up in a parcel.

Those children who stayed behind in the towns found their schools closed.

This girl is waiting for a train
to take her away from London.

**"I hated putting on my gas mask –
I felt I couldn't breathe."**

Look at this little girl wearing her
gas mask. Look for the breathing
holes.

London 1940

Everyone had to carry a gas mask
in case poison gas was dropped
by the enemy.

Things to do

Start to make a book about what it was like in the war.
Call the book *Children in the Second World War*.

Talk to people who were born in the 1930s. How old were they when the war
began? Ask them if they were evacuated. Write down what they tell you.

Look on a map to find Germany.

Blackout and security

Look at the Air Raid Warden. He looked after people in air raids. What do you think he is doing?

"If there was a slither of light showing, the air raid warden shouted 'Put out that light!'"

All lights had to be hidden after dark so that enemy planes would not know where to drop bombs. Windows of houses, trains, buses, schools and factories were covered up. There were no street lights.

"When we came out of the pictures it was inky black. We put our hands out in front to feel our way."

4

"At the seaside barbed wire and big concrete cubes blocked the beach."

In 1940 Germany was preparing to invade Britain. Road blocks and sandbags were used. Roads and beaches were guarded by men who hid in concrete pill-boxes.

Signposts were taken away so that the Germans would not know which way to go.

Look at all the signposts stacked away.

Everyone had an identity card.

"We were told never to speak to strangers in case they were spies."

Things to do

Ask someone over 40 what they remember about the blackout.
What was it like at the seaside? What was an identity card?
Write down what you find out.

Look for old sea defences, pill-boxes or gunsites near where you live.

The Home Guard

Maidenhead, Berkshire 1940

The Home Guard guarded the railways, the cliffs
and lonely spots where the Germans might land.

**"My husband joined the Home Guard while he was at school.
He went into the army when he was old enough."**

Look at the photograph of some men of the Home Guard.
At first the Home Guard had no weapons or uniforms.
Look at the Sunbeam car they have made into an armoured car.

"A German plane was shot down near us. One of the Home Guard went with a pitchfork to capture the pilot. The German put his hands up."

Hale, near Fordingbridge, Hampshire 1940

Look at this German plane which has crashed in a garden.
Look for:

—the soldier guarding the plane
—the Swastika sign on the tail. This shows it was a German plane.
—the damaged house.

Things to do

Ask people who were children in the war about the Home Guard.
Was it like "Dad's Army"? Write down what they tell you.

Look for steel helmets, badges, arm bands and other Home Guard relics.

Air raids

**"We heard the German planes above us.
They sounded different from ours.
They went 'oom-oom'. We were frightened."**

Enemy planes dropped bombs on London and other
big cities. Some bombs blew up houses.
Some started fires.

Look at the stirrup pump, water and sand for putting out fires.

**"I was taken up a hill near Hitchin to watch
London burning 34 miles** (55 km) **away."**

Anti-aircraft guns tried to shoot down the raiders.
Searchlights raked the sky. Fighter planes chased
the enemy raiders. Big balloons hung in the sky.

Southampton 1941

**"We used to see who could
collect the biggest piece
of shrapnel."**

Look at this newspaper lady selling
papers after her shop had been bombed.

**"I heard 1,000 bombers on their
way to Germany. I felt a bit
sorry for the Germans."**

Things to do

Talk to someone who was bombed at work or at home.
Were they frightened? Write down what they tell you.

Where did the shrapnel come from?

Draw an Air Raid Warden putting out a fire with a stirrup pump.

Shelters

"My brother was sent to Kent in 1940. He watched dog-fights in the sky. It was the Battle of Britain."

Look at these children watching the fighter planes. They are sheltering in a slit trench, because there was no proper shelter.

Left: Kent 1940

Some people had an Anderson shelter in their garden. It was made of curved pieces of iron.

These people were in the shelter when a bomb landed.

"It was cold and damp in the shelter. Sometimes it flooded, but it was better than being buried under the house."

10

"My cousin was asleep in the house. He was killed. His brothers and sisters tore their fingers trying to reach him under the rubble."

In London the safest place was deep in the Underground. People went down to the Underground stations to spend the night. Look for:

— the name of the station
— the people looking for
   a place to sit
— the girl with her knitting
— the mother with her baby.

London Underground 1940

Things to do

Ask someone over 40 how they sheltered in an air raid.

Look for old shelters in back gardens. See if there are any brick shelters near where you live.

Salvage

Children went round collecting waste paper, jam jars, bones, cardboard, rags and scrap metal to make into weapons.

Look at these boys collecting salvage. It will be taken away to make part of a gun, ship or tank.

"Workmen took away iron railings from gardens, parks and houses. They took the railing from our chapel."

Blean, near Canterbury, Kent 1942

These children are outside their school. Look for:

— the posters asking people to save
— the paper crosses on the windows. They were put there to stop the glass breaking during an air raid.

Here is a tank factory where men and women worked day and night.

"There was a factory near us that made Spitfires. Saucepans were collected to get aluminium to make aeroplanes."

N E England 1942

Things to do

Talk to someone who was at school during the war. Ask if they collected salvage. Did they have savings stamps? Write down what they tell you in your book.

Draw your own poster asking people to save to buy weapons.

Food

Enemy submarines tried to stop food coming to Britain.
People were told to "Dig for victory" — to grow more food.
Playing fields and parks were ploughed up to grow vegetables.

"In September we had two weeks' holiday to help with potato picking."

Look at these boys helping the farmer.

Left: Ripon, Yorkshire 1942

Some women joined the Land Army and worked on farms.

To make sure there was enough food to go round, each person had a ration book. The shopkeeper cut out the coupons and gave a share of food. You still had to pay!

**"You could get whale meat 'off the ration'.
It tasted of cod liver oil."**

Each person was allowed 8 ounces (200 grams) of sweets every four weeks.
    People queued to get some extra treat. Sometimes shopkeepers would keep something "under the counter" for a favourite customer.

Look at this old lady coming out of a shop.
She has one egg in her hand.

London 1941

Things to do

Ask someone over 40 about food at school and at home when they were your age. Ask if they helped with the harvest. Write down what they tell you.

See if you can find an old ration book.
How many Mars bars would you have been able to get for one month's ration?

Look for a wartime recipe.

Clothes and travel

You had to give coupons
for clothes too.
At some schools there
was a clothes exchange
where you could swop
clothes.

Look at these children
trying clothes to see if
they are the right size.

**"You could buy
dusters without
coupons. My mother
made me a blouse
out of three dusters."**

Army blankets were made
into coats for children.
Clothes were cut down
and remade. It was
called make-do-and-mend.

London 1940

16

"I never got a seat on the train. It was always crowded with soldiers."

To save petrol and coal, people were asked not to travel. There was no petrol for family cars. A lot of people cycled.

Look at this poster which tells people to walk whenever possible.

Go by SHANKS' PONY

Walk short distances
AND LEAVE ROOM FOR THOSE WHO HAVE LONGER JOURNEYS

Things to do

Ask someone who remembers the war to tell you about clothes rationing. Ask them how they travelled in wartime.
Did the trains stop if there was an air raid? Write down what they tell you.

Amusements and toys

There was no television. People listened to the radio instead.
For factory workers there was a programme called "Music while
you work".

**"ITMA was a funny
programme that made
us laugh and forget
the war."**

Look at this copy of
the "Beano". It is dated
1 February 1941.

There were favourite
songs that people hummed,
whistled or sang.

**"A lot of the songs
were sad, but I liked
'Roll out the barrel'
and 'Run rabbit run'
the best."**

"I was collecting metal farm animals from Woolworth's but after the war started you couldn't get them any more."

People learned to make toys from scraps of wood and odds and ends.

Look at this soldier painting a toy horse he has made.

"I had a nice cloth doll with a painted face and hair made of wool."

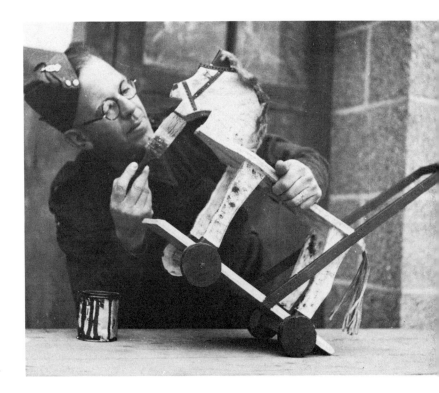

Military Hospital, Moretonhampstead, Devon 1943

Things to do

See if you can find the words to wartime songs. Write them down.
Ask someone who remembers these songs to sing one to you.
Ask about ITMA. What did the letters stand for?
What toys did they have in the war? Write down what you find out.

See if you can design a simple wooden toy or cloth doll.

Americans

In January 1942 American soldiers came to Britain.
They built new airfields and began to fly planes to bomb Germany.

**"We liked the Americans. At Christmas they collected all
the children from the villages round about. They took us to a party
at their camp. We had ice cream, nice food and a film."**

Look at these two little
girls. One of them
has been given a present
by some American soldiers.

All the countries on Britain's side were called the Allies.
They were France, America, Russia, Poland, Canada, Australia, New Zealand,
Norway, Holland and Belgium. Germany, Italy and Japan were on
the other side.

In June 1944 the Allies were ready to land in France
to attack the Germans.

**"There were lots of soldiers camped in the New Forest.
They were waiting to go on the ships. On the day they left
they threw sweets and pennies for us to catch."**

Look at the truck
full of soldiers.
Look for:

— the girl touching
   the soldier's hand
— the star painted on
   the side of the truck.
   It showed they were on
   their way to France.

London 1944

Things to do

Ask someone over 40 if they met any Americans during the war.

Look on a map to find where the countries of our allies are.
Draw a map in your book. Mark on it the countries who were allies.

Find out where the Allied Forces landed in France in 1944.

Victory

The Germans made one last attempt to win the war. They sent
hundreds of flying bombs and rockets over to London
and the south of England. They caused terrible damage.

**"With some of them you had no warning. They made no sound.
One Saturday afternoon one fell on Woolworth's at Lewisham,
quite near us. Our neighbours were killed."**

This house has been hit
by a flying bomb.
Look for:

— the Air Raid Wardens with "W"
   on their tin hats
— the child being rescued
— the warden going up the ladder
   for more people.

**"I remember the dust that filled
the air after an explosion,
and the strange smell after the
bomb fell."**

All the efforts of the Germans failed.
In 1945 they were defeated.

The war was over. The church bells rang out for victory.

"The street parties, bonfires and singsongs were great. We were all so happy that it was over."

These children are enjoying a street party.

Look for:

— the paper hats worn by the children
— the food. There is not much to eat because food was rationed.

Finsbury Park, London 1945

The lights were on again. No more blackout!

"It seemed all wrong to see the lights streaming out from our windows."

Things to do

Ask someone over 40 about flying bombs. What did people call them?

Look for a War Memorial near where you live. Read the names of the people who did not come back from the war.

Look for family photographs, letters and diaries from the war years.

Draw a picture of a street party.

After the war

Not everyone was happy.

**"My dad never came back from the war.
He was killed in a battle on a beach
in Italy."**

London 1941

The following museums have displays of relics from the Second World War:

Imperial War Museum, Lambeth Road, London
Norfolk Rural Museum, Beech House, Gressenhall, Dereham, Norfolk
Museum of London, London Wall
Duxford Airfield, Duxford, Cambridge
The Tank Museum, Bovington Camp, Wareham, Dorset

There are service museums in most parts of Britain.

Visit one near where you live.

At home in the 1950s

Shirley Echlin

Longman

Contents

Melbourn, Cambridgeshire 1954

Outside the home

Harlow, Essex 1957

Look at this photograph. The houses on the left are terraced houses.
Each one is joined to the house next door. The large building
on the right is divided into flats. Several families live in
this building.

Look for:

— the balconies in the flats
— the garages in a row, by the flats
— the trees and bushes
— the television aerials.

**"We lived in a new terraced house. The walls were not very thick.
We could hear someone playing the piano from two houses away."**

2

Look at this photograph of a new house. It was built over 30 years ago. The outside walls have plaster over the bricks.

Materials for building new houses were difficult to get in the early 1950s. Timber and steel were rationed.

"Bricks had to be ordered at least one year before you needed them."

Throckley, Northumberland 1951

Things to do

Start to make a book about life *At home in the 1950s.* Find some houses or flats near where you live that were built in the 1950s.
Draw a picture or take a photograph of them. Stick the picture in your book.

Talk to someone over 30 about the new houses that were built in the 1950s. Write down what they tell you.

Inside the home

Harlow, Essex 1955

**"We loved our new house. Everything was light and airy.
After living in a converted Nissen hut, it was marvellous
to be warm and dry."**

Look at this photograph of a sitting room.

Look for:

— the fireplace which burns coal
— the piano
— the armchairs which have wooden armrests and spaces in the frames.
  Furniture in the 1950s was lighter in colour and weighed less.
— the size and shape of the table legs
— the patterns on the vases. They were designed to go with
  the new furniture.
— the venetian blind at the window.

These plates were bought in the 1950s. Look at the leaf pattern.

Many new ideas for objects in the house were first shown at the 1951 Festival of Britain. This powder compact had face powder in it. Look for the date.

"I went on a school outing to the Festival of Britain in London. It was very exciting to see the new things that were being made."

Things to do

Draw a picture of your sitting room. Is the furniture in your room different or the same as the furniture in the photograph?

Ask an adult if they have objects in their home from the 1950s. Perhaps they will allow you to draw these objects. Write underneath your drawings anything they tell you about these things.

Radio

Most homes in the 1950s had a radio. It worked by having
its plug put into an electric socket on the wall.

**"If our radio ever went wrong, my Dad used to fix it.
He'd take off the back. Inside were large metal things
like upside down bottles called valves."**

This is a picture of
a radio called a
wireless.

Pye Fen Man radio 1955

Look for:

— the four plastic knobs.
   These were used
   to switch the radio
   on and off. They were
   also used to find
   different programmes.
— the two speakers above
   the knobs where the
   sound came from
— the air vent at the
   side to stop the radio
   getting too hot
   inside.

This photograph shows three men making a radio programme.
Their programme was very funny. It was called "The Goon Show".
The men's names (from left to right) are Peter Sellers, Harry Secombe and Spike Milligan.

"The Goon Show", BBC Home Service 1960

**"I never missed 'The Goon Show'.
My favourite person in the show was called Bluebottle.
I could copy his funny voice."**

Things to do

Compare the size of the wireless with a transistor radio in your home. Find out why your radio is smaller.

Ask an adult to tell you about their favourite radio programme in the 1950s. How often did they listen to the radio? Write down what they tell you.

Television

"We were so excited when we had our first telly. The picture was black and white. We watched everything. It was like going to the cinema every day."

A television set was an expensive item to buy. Most families did not have a television in their home in the early 1950s. It was something you might watch in a friend's home if they were wealthy enough to own a television. Later in the 1950s, more families bought television sets.

Right:
Pye television
set 1949

Christopher Trace and Leila Williams were the first presenters of a new children's television programme. It was called "Blue Peter".

**"I loved Muffin the Mule.
He was so sweet. I even had
a puppet exactly like Muffin.
It was a Christmas present."**

The puppet in this photograph became
a famous television character. He was
called Muffin the Mule. The woman at
the top made the puppet move by
pulling the strings. The other woman
talked to the puppet and played
the piano. Muffin danced on top of
the piano.

BBC television 1952

Things to do

Look carefully at the clothes worn by the presenters of "Blue Peter".
Do they look different from those worn by the people who present
"Blue Peter" now? Make a list of the differences in your book.

Draw a picture of Muffin the Mule. Then draw beside it a picture
of a puppet from a children's television programme today.

The kitchen

"It was the first time I had hot water from the tap."

Families wanted to have kitchens that were easy to use. New equipment was bought so that less time was spent on the jobs in the kitchen.

Refrigerators kept food fresh for a long time. Now shopping did not have to be done every day.

Olympia 1955

10

This type of refrigerator was made so that it could work on gas, electricity or paraffin. This one worked on paraffin.

Look carefully at the photograph.

Look for:

— the paraffin container at the bottom
— the small size of the part that kept the food cold
— the ice tray.

Electrolux refrigerator 1950

"If my fridge stopped working, I just tipped it on one side. I could hear the liquid moving around inside. Anyway, whatever it was I did, the fridge always started to work again."

Things to do

Make two lists in your book. Call one list *Kitchens then.* Write about kitchens and kitchen equipment in the 1950s. Call the other list *Kitchens now.* Write about kitchens today.

Washday

"My washing machine made the job of washing the clothes much easier. It was quicker too."

Look at the photograph of a woman washing a football team's kit. The washing machine is made of steel. Can you see the wringer on the top of the machine? The rollers squeezed the water out of the wet clothes.

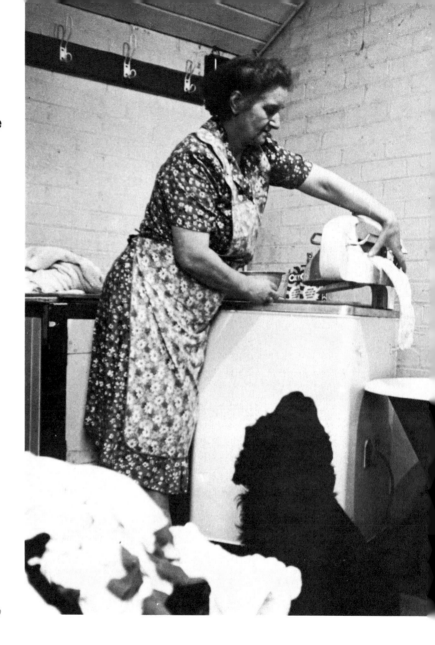

Colchester, Essex 1950

Before the 1950s, washing machines had to be filled with water that was already hot. The washing machine in the photograph worked by electricity. Electric heaters were fitted to the washing tub. Cold water was put in the machine and heated by the electric heater.

12

1 Sort whites, coloureds, and woollens while filling the Parnall All-Electric Safety Washer by the flexible hose which will fit your hot-water tap. (There is a Parnall model that will boil the water too!)

60 minute washday!

2 Load Washer with clothes . . . and switch on . . .

4 Reload the Washer with more dirty clothes and whilst these are being washed, rinse and wring the first load through the Parnall Safety Power Wringer . . .

3 Time for a "cuppa" while the Washer gently but thoroughly washes the clothes by unique Parnall "washing-swirl" action . . .

5 Just one hour gone and a week's average family wash is out on the line . . . clean and fine. Then let the Parnall empty itself — by power.

PARNALL

ALL-ELECTRIC · World's Best Safety Washer

£65 · 2 · 0 TAX PAID—or with Water Heater **£75 · 12 · 0**
— *and really easy terms*

SEE ONE AT YOUR LOCAL DEALER'S OR ELECTRICITY SHOWROOMS

Parnall (Yate) Ltd., 255 North Circular Road, Neasden, London, N.W.10
WHG P.33

Advertisement 1955

This is an advertisement for a washing machine.

Look for:

— the time the makers claim it will take to do the washing

— the prices. Could you buy a new washing machine for that price today?

"I bent down to get the wet clothes out of the washing machine. My little girl thought she'd help. She started the power ringer and caught my hair in the rollers. It did hurt."

Things to do

Find out how much time a load of clothes takes to wash today. Write this time down. Compare this with the time in the advertisement.

Are your wet clothes hung on a line to dry?

Ask someone over 30 if they remember their first electric washing machine.

13

Boys' and girls' clothes

"Boys always wore short trousers. I didn't get my first long pair until I was thirteen. My knees got very sore and chapped during the winter."

These boys are playing a game called "Weak 'orses". How do you think it was played?

Look for:

— the length of the short trousers. Look at the length of the short trousers that boys wear now.
— the long woollen socks
— the overcoats
— the boots
— the boy's cap.

London

"I used to spend hours ironing my daughter's summer dresses. It was really hard to iron out the creases."

Look at the photograph of the three girls. The girl in the middle came from Jamaica. Many West Indian families came to Britain to get work in the 1950s.

Brixton, London 1952

Look for:

— the girls' dresses. Do girls always wear dresses in the summer now?
— the canvas sandals worn by the girl on the left. They had to be cleaned with whitener.

Things to do

Ask an adult if they remember any of their favourite clothes that they wore when they were your age. Ask them to describe these clothes. Perhaps they could show you some photographs of themselves.

Draw a picture of a boy and a girl from the 1950s.

Toys, comics and books

"I played a great game. I was Davy Crockett with my fur hat. I would pretend to track my mates who were the Indians."

Many toys were based on characters in films and comics. This picture shows a boy dressed up in a Dan Dare space suit.

Below: London 1951

London 1954

This boy is playing with a toy horse. It was called a Mobo Horse. You sat on the saddle and pushed down. The horse would then move forwards.

"I had a baby doll. All it did was cry and blink its eyes."

Here are some comics and annuals from the 1950s.

"I had the 'Girls' Crystal' magazine each week and the annual each Christmas. I loved the stories about schoolgirls in boarding schools."

Look at some of these words that were used in comics and annuals:

"Wizard idea! Golly!"
"It was a silly jape."
"The cunning bounder."
"The chums rushed to the rescue."

Things to do

Talk to several adults. Ask them to tell you about their favourite toys, comics and books. Make a list of them in your book. Can you buy any of these comics or annuals now?

Visit your local museum. Find out if they have an old toys' exhibition.

Plastics

Plastic was used more and more in the home. It was easy to clean and it did not weigh much.

**"I used to spend two hours putting on my make-up.
I wanted to look glamorous."**

**"I used to buy Airspun Face Powder by Coty. It cost
5 shillings** (25p). **My mum gave me a Toni Home Perm.
The smell of the perm lotion was terrible."**

Look carefully at
the photograph of
a plastic make-up bag.

Look for:

— the plastic jars and
   bottle with screw-top
   lids
— the fluffy powder puff
— the quilted plastic
   material with a flower
   pattern on it.

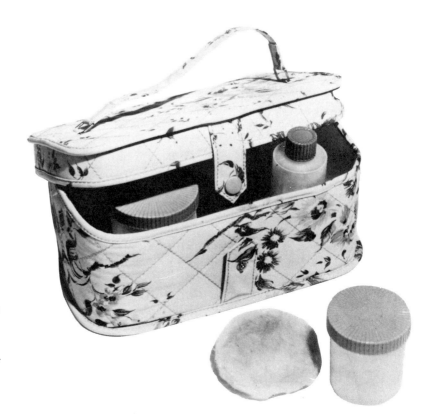

**"I went dancing twice a week.
The new music was rock and roll."**

Plastic was used to make records.
More and more people bought records
in the 1950s.

Look again at page 10. Look for
the things made from plastic
in the kitchen.

Things to do

Ask an adult where they liked to go when they went out.
Did they enjoy dancing? What sort of music did they
listen to? Write down what they tell you in your book.

Listen to an old rock and roll record.

Collect items made of plastic that were made in the 1950s.

Coronation day

On 2 June 1953
Queen Elizabeth II
was crowned.
All over Britain,
people had their own
celebrations at home.
Some people had a
street party for
the children.

*Bethnal Green,
London 1953*

**"I ate so much cake and jelly that I made myself sick.
I had a red, white and blue paper hat. We had a huge
Union Jack hanging from my bedroom window."**

Look carefully at the photograph above of a street party.
Look at the number of men wearing suits. Look for the party hats
and the flags. Can you see any television aerials?

These children are singing and dancing. They are giving this performance to celebrate the Queen being crowned. These children lived in a street in London. People who lived there collected money for 10 months. Then they had enough money for a street party and entertainment.

London 1953

Things to do

Go to your local library. Find a book which has photographs of Queen Elizabeth II being crowned.

Ask several adults if a street party was held in their street to celebrate the Coronation. Find out if they own a special Coronation mug.

Imagine you were at a Coronation street party in 1953. Write about what happened.

Shopping

In the early 1950s, every member of a family had a food ration book. The shopkeeper used to cut out coupons from these books. This would allow each family to buy a certain amount of food. Even sweets were rationed.

"Shopping took hours. My feet used to ache from queuing. I was fed up with rationing."

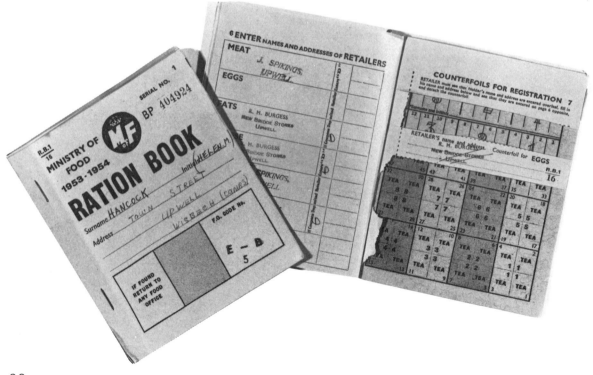

Harlow, Essex 1953

Look carefully at the photograph above. It shows a shopping centre in a new town.

Look for:

— the people queuing for bread
— the man wearing trousers that come down just below the knees. These are called "plus fours".
— the motor bike with side car
— the high pram
— the ladies wearing headscarves
— the long coats.

Things to do

Ask someone over 30 what they remember about shops and shopping when they were your age. Write down what you find out.

In 1952, each person was allowed 14 ounces (395 grams) of meat each week. The price of this was 1 shilling and 9 old pence (9p). Find out how much meat your family eats each week now. How much does your meat cost?

At home

This mother is busy knitting and her two daughters are looking at a book. Perhaps the mother has finished all her jobs in the house. Look at her headscarf. This was to keep her hair clean.

Harlow, Essex 1950

Would you have enjoyed living in a home like this in the 1950s?

Most towns have some housing estates that were built in the 1950s. Is there one near where you live?

The following New Towns were built in the 1950s. Some of them have museums.

Basildon, Essex
Bracknell, Berkshire
Corby, Northamptonshire
Crawley, Sussex
Cumbernauld, Strathclyde
Cwmbran, Gwent
East Kilbride, Strathclyde

Glenrothes, Fife
Harlow, Essex
Hatfield, Hertfordshire
Hemel Hempstead, Hertfordshire
Newton Aycliffe, County Durham
Peterlee, County Durham
Welwyn Garden City, Hertfordshire

Only a few of these towns have begun to collect photographs of their early history. Perhaps you can help by collecting photographs and objects yourself.

At school in the 1950s

Sallie Purkis

Longman

Contents

*Brooklands School,
Greenwich, London 1958*

New schools

Albrighton School, Shropshire

After the end of the Second World War, many new babies were born.
It was called a "baby boom". By 1950, these children were old enough
to go to school. More schools were needed. New schools were built
on new housing estates and in New Towns.

**"Our school was only one of five new schools built at that time.
It was part of a big building programme."**

Look at the school in the photograph.

Look for:

— the flat roof
— the large windows
— the builder's plank by the main entrance.

2

"I was one of the first pupils at the school. I remember the day it opened for the first time."

This photograph shows a crowded school hall. Look at the children and visitors. They are there for the opening of a new school. Can you see the mayor?

Forster School, Lewisham, London 1952

Things to do

Start to make a book about schools in the 1950s. Call the first page *New Schools*.
Find a school near where you live, like the ones in the photographs.
Draw a picture or take a photograph of it. Try to find someone who can
tell you about when a school opened. Write down what they tell you.

If your school is an old school, look carefully round the building.
Were any new parts built in the 1950s?

Inside school

Kingswood School, Basildon, Essex 1957

"The school was light and airy.
All round it was green grass and garden.
I had never taught in such a marvellous building before."

Here is a photograph of
the teachers at a school
30 years ago. Notice
that the women teachers
are not wearing trousers.

St Francis de Sales School, London

The new schools had extra rooms that older schools did not have.

"We had a large central hall, inside lavatories, a staff room, kitchen and dining room."

Look at this photograph
of children reading
in their classroom.
Working in small
groups was a new
idea in the 1950s.

Essendon School, Hertfordshire 1949

Things to do

Talk to a teacher who worked in an old school but moved
to a new school. What was different about the new school?
Write down what they tell you in your book.

Draw a plan of your school. Write on it the names of each room.

The classroom

Here is a class of boys in their new classroom.

Look for:

— the large windows

— the desks with a shelf underneath, arranged in rows

— the handwriting exercise on the blackboard.

— the loudspeaker on the wall in the photograph.

   Sometimes the children listened to Schools Radio programmes.

"The master radio was in the office.

There were speakers in every room.

You plugged in in your classroom if you wanted to listen."

"The ballpoint pen had just come in. It was the end of the old pen and ink."

These older girls had locker desks. They were new in the 1950s.

Dee House Ursuline Convent School, Chester 1956

"Mine was always untidy. It was so nice to have somewhere to keep all our things."

Things to do

Look round your school. What sort of desks do you have?
How are they arranged? Is it the same or different from the 1950s?

Ask your head teacher if there are any photographs like these
of your school.

Draw a picture of a new classroom in the 1950s.

School clothes

All Saints School, Farnworth, Lancashire 1954

These children went to an old school in 1954. It has
now been pulled down.

Look for:

— the boys in short trousers
— the girls in skirts with straps
— the short hair cuts of the boys
— the girls' hair tied with ribbon
— the children with National Health glasses.

**"I loved to choose my hair ribbon each morning.
I matched the colour to the rest of my clothes.
Under our skirts we wore navy blue knickers."**

Some schools had a uniform.
The children wore a school tie
and a school badge on their
blazer pocket. Look at the girl
in her school uniform.

**"We didn't insist on it, but they
could wear it if they liked."**

Things to do

In your book write the heading *School clothes*.
Look at what your teachers and other children in your class
wear to school. How have things changed since the 1950s?
Draw some pictures and write about what you notice.

Collect some old school photographs. Compare them with
a photograph of your class now.

Find out about the National Health Service.

School milk

Every child was given
a free bottle of milk
each day. At playtime
the milk and straws
were given out.

"I liked being
the milk monitor.
I had to put the
straws in the bottles.
We saved the milk
tops to buy guide
dogs for the blind."

Deansfield School, London 1963

10

Many new school kitchens were built in the 1950s. Dinners were cooked for other schools in the neighbourhood.

"We all had a hot dinner served through the hatch. At half past eleven each day, a van drew up. It took meals from our kitchen in containers to other people."

Caldecot School, Denmark Hill, London 1951

Things to do

Write the heading *Food and drink* in your book.
What did children eat and drink at school 30 years ago?
What happens in your school now?

Find out how many children in your school have a hot meal at school and how many bring food from home. Write down what you find out.

Streaming

There was more competition in schools in the 1950s than there is today.

"We had marks for attendance and marks for tests. Everyone had a position in class."

Look at this school report.

Look for:

— the number in class
— the attendance number
— the different subjects
— the teacher's comments

Name: Stephen Attmore   Class: 3A1   Number in Class: 39
Position in Exam: 3/6   Attendance: 355/369   Times Late:

Subject	Marks Poss.	Marks Obt.	Grade	Teachers' Comments
Arithmetic:				
(a) Mental	20	17		} Very good progress
(b) Mechanical	40	38		} has been made.
(c) Problems	40	33		
English:				
(a) Comprehension	20	20		} Very good work has
(b) Composition	40	37		been done in this subject
(c) Spelling	10	9½		Compositions are
(d) General	30	22½		always interesting.
(e) Spoken				
TOTAL	200	177		
History			V.G.	Shows lively interest,
Geography			G.	especially in Nature
Nature Study or Science			V.G.	Study. Has done very
Scripture			V.G.	good written work & illustrations
Art			G.	
Craft or Needlework			G.	Has worked well.
Music			G.	Has shown great keenness.
Physical Training			V.G.	Very keen & alert.

Grading: V.G.—Very Good; G.—Good; Av.—Average; W.—Weak; U.—Unsatisfactory.

GENERAL REMARKS:—

Stephen has good ability & is good, conscientious worker in all subjects.

Report received and noted: Class Teacher: D Gillson

B.L. Attmore   Headmaster: E.T. Wood
Parent or Guardian.   Next term begins on September 10.

Children were put into different classes called "streams". Those who did well in tests went into the A class. The other children went into the B class.

"All the classes were streamed from the first year in the Juniors. Once you were put in a class it was very unusual to change. You went up the school like that."

At the end of the fourth year all the children sat an examination. It was called the "Eleven Plus" or scholarship. Those who passed it went to one sort of school. The children who didn't pass went to another sort of school. More children failed than passed.

"My parents bought me a bike for passing the scholarship, but I wasn't as happy as they were. I went on a bus to my new school. Most of my friends went to one nearer home."

Things to do

Make two lists in your book. Call one list *School Competition Now.*
Write down what competitions you have at school.
Call the other list *School Competition Then.*
Write down what competition was for in the 1950s.

Talk to someone who sat the "Eleven Plus" or scholarship.
What was it like?

Try to borrow some old school reports.

Lessons

All Saints School, Farnworth, Lancashire 1954

Some teachers had new ideas 30 years ago.
They wanted the children to work on their own
for some of the time.

14

Look at this photograph of a school shop.
These children are learning mathematics in a new way.
The teacher is nowhere in sight.

Look for:

— the boxes and tins collected by the class
— the boy who is being shopkeeper
— the customers in the queue
— the girl and boy with the box of chocolates.

The children were taught different subjects.
Each subject had a time on the timetable.

"Mental arithmetic every morning, with always some formal English to follow. History and geography were separate subjects. We read a chapter in a book."

Things to do

Talk to someone who sat the "Eleven Plus" or scholarship. What was it like?
What were the old ideas? What were the new ones?
Write down what they tell you in your book.

What sort of lessons do you have today?

Draw a picture of a mathematics lesson 30 years ago.

Music, art and craft

London 1952

"On Fridays we had percussion band. The teacher said,
'Keep your eyes on the conductor.' If one person
played too soon, it was spoilt for all the rest."

Look at this photograph of children playing musical instruments.

Look for:

— the boy who is being the conductor
— the triangles
— the two girls with different instruments.

Can you find the boy who will make a mistake?

16

The new schools had sinks in the classrooms. More painting was possible in schools in the 1950s. Craft was often called handwork or handicraft. Models had to be carefully measured.

"Once a week we had craft. Boys and girls were taught separately. Boys learnt to use tools and a ruler. They made models of card and wood. Girls turned their hands to needlework."

Brockley Road School, London 1951

Things to do

Ask someone older than 30 about music lessons when they were your age.
What instruments did they play? What tunes do they remember?
Write down what they tell you in your book.

Draw a picture of the girls' sewing class.

Do you think girls and boys should learn different things?
Write down your answer in your book.

PE and dance

**"It seemed so big at first. I made myself climb
a bit higher each week till I reached the top."**

These children are
swinging on the apparatus.
They have changed their
clothes for PE. This was
all new in the 1950s.
When their mothers and
fathers went to school,
there was very little
PE equipment.

**"We wanted them all to have plimsolls.
We didn't want ordinary shoes on the new floor."**

"Country dancing was always popular. 'Rufty Tufty', 'Gathering Peascods' and 'Durham Reel' were those I liked best. The teacher called out above the music to remind us of what to do next."

The music was played on a piano or came from a record. Sometimes they had country dancing as one of the lessons. Sometimes it was after school.

George Eliot School, London 1953

Things to do

Find out about PE lessons by talking to someone who was at school 30 years ago. Then talk to someone who was at school 60 years ago. Write down what they tell you in your book.

Draw some pictures to show the differences.

Ask your teacher to let you try country dancing.

Other sports

St Francis de Sales School, London

Children at a new school in the 1950s played sports and games on the field behind their school. Those at older schools went to a field nearby to play.

"There were teams for every sport. Most people had a chance to play in something while they were at the school. My school won the Junior Schools' Shield several times."

"We started the annual sports day in 1952. Everyone had a lot of fun. It was quite a novelty then to have the mothers taking part."

Below is a photograph of mothers racing at a school sports.

Above and left: Arbury School, Cambridge 1960

Look for:

— the women's dresses
— the petticoat worn by one mother
— the woman wearing trousers.

Things to do

Look at the team photographs. There is one here and one on the back cover. Is the kit they wore the same as teams wear today? What is different?

Ask your teacher to look for some old team photographs.

Write about a girl whose mother won the mothers' race.

Special days

Albrighton School, Shropshire 1953

Most schools had one or two special days a year.
Sometimes the children went out. Sometimes visitors
came in. Every school celebrated the Coronation of
Queen Elizabeth II in June 1953.

The children in this photograph took part in an Elizabethan pageant.
They dressed up like people who lived at the time of the first
Queen Elizabeth.

Look for:

— the girl who is being the Queen. She has a hoop inside her skirt.
— the boy with the fancy cloak
— the three children with their feet in the stocks. They cannot
  get out until the stocks are unlocked.

At this school, they decided to plant a small tree. It is a big tree now.

ROYALTY IN ESSEX

A SOUVENIR BOOK
FOR ESSEX CHILDREN
PRESENTED BY
THE COUNTY COUNCIL OF ESSEX
ON THE OCCASION OF THE CORONATION OF
HER MAJESTY QUEEN ELIZABETH II.
ON JUNE 2ND. 1953

Most children were given a gift for the Coronation. Many had Coronation mugs. Here is a book given to children in Essex.

Things to do

Ask someone older than 30 to look through their photograph albums.
Have they any pictures taken at the time of the Coronation?
Ask them what they did at school on special days.

Try to borrow a Coronation mug or cup.

Perhaps your school celebrated the Queen's Silver Jubilee in 1978.
Write down what children at school did in 1953 and what you did 25 years later.

School 30 years ago

All Saints School, Farnworth, Lancashire 1954

This school play was called "The Magic Button". It was put on in 1954. The children in the photograph have all grown up. Their own children are at school now. This photograph is part of the history of the school.

Can you make a collection of photographs about your school?

Most towns have some housing estates and schools that were built in the 1950s. The following New Towns were built in the 1950s. Some of them have museums.

Basildon, Essex
Bracknell, Berkshire
Corby, Northamptonshire
Crawley, Sussex
Cumbernauld, Strathclyde
Cwmbran, Gwent
East Kilbride, Strathclyde

Glenrothes, Fife
Harlow, Essex
Hatfield, Hertfordshire
Hemel Hempstead, Hertfordshire
Newton Aycliffe, County Durham
Peterlee, County Durham
Welwyn Garden City, Hertfordshire

Only a few of these towns have begun to collect photographs of their early history. Perhaps you can help by collecting photographs and objects yourself.

Index

At school in the 1950s

Children and history

These books aim to introduce children to history by using as a starting point, places and people familiar to them.

Although the Second World War and the 1950s may not seem like history to adults, this is a long time ago to children.

This book was compiled from information collected by children talking to people who remember the War and the 1950s. The photographs were added later. Oral history can be used in three ways:
a) you can play children a tape recording you have made
b) you can invite someone elderly to answer the children's questions
c) the children collect their own information using either a tape recorder or a written questionnaire.

In this last way, children can provide resources for their own project.

Projects on the Second World War and the 1950s involving oral history are particularly worthwhile. The projects could emphasise ordinary people's participation in the making of history and reflect both local and national changes. These could include:
— evacuation and air raids
— life in a New Town
— the Festival of Britain
— the Coronation of Queen Elizabeth II.

There are photographs and artefacts in both public and private collections. The children can build up an archive by collecting photographs and objects themselves. Some local libraries and Record Offices will be pleased to see the photographs and may wish to take copies for permanent preservation.